INSIDE IMPROVISATION

VOL. 4 «MELODIC RHYTHMS»

JERRY BERGONZI

Edited by Geraldine Bergonzi.

Music typesetting: Thomas M. Zentawer

Cover design: Traugott Bratic

Cover photo: Gildas Boclé

Printed in Germany.

Production: Hans Gruber

Published by Advance Music.

ADV 14261

Table of Contents

CD Track List

TRACK	TUNE	C INSTRUMENTS - PAGE	B♭ INSTRUMENTS - PAGE	E♭ INSTRUMENTS - PAGE
1	Tuning notes (A Concert)			
2	Tuning notes (B♭ Concert)			
3, 4	1 ♦ *Sleep Walk*	11	12	13
5, 6	2 ♦ *Wine Tasting*	17	18	19
7, 8	3 ♦ *Together Alone*	35	36	37
9, 10	4 ♦ *It's No One But You*	41	42	43
11, 12	5 ♦ *It Happened*	53	54	55
13, 14	6 ♦ *Into Somewhere*	68	69	70
15, 16	7 ♦ *Come and Gone*	77	78	79
17, 18	8 ♦ *One Heart*	82	83	84
19, 20	9 ♦ *Twinkle Twinkle*	91	92	93
21, 22	10 ♦ *There Is Another You*	110	111	112
23	Demonstrating 3 notes over the bar			
24	Demonstrating different numbers of consecutive triplets			
25	Playing 3/4, 5/4 and 7/4 rhythms over 4/4			
26	Playing polyrhythms: 5 over 2			
27	Demonstrating different rhythmic devices			
28	Demonstrating different rhythmic devices			
29	Demonstrating different rhythmic devices			

Introduction

Time and rhythm are king! Number one! We are constantly made aware of this fact when we are playing or listening to improvised music. All notes seem to sound good when they are played with "good time." Even melodies that use "wrong" notes or notes that aren't in the chord seem to sound good when played with good time. And so it is that "good" notes played with mediocre time sound only mediocre at best.

When we say that a particular player has a "great feel" we are usually referring to one's "time feel," that is, how that player expresses the time. "Laid back," "on top," "swinging," "a good groove," are all terms that describe the personality of how someone plays the time. It's difficult to talk about personality, to say with words why someone has a good time feel. What often packages or dresses up a good time feel are the rhythms a particular artist chooses to use. This book hopefully lends some insight into practicing and playing creative rhythms in a melodic fashion. Often jazz educators present improvisation techniques by first teaching which notes to play and then describing how to put these notes to various rhythms. There is a profound difference in taking rhythms and then applying the notes to those particular rhythms.

Rhythms are inexhaustible. These upcoming chapters hope to expand your rhythmic vocabulary by presenting various rhythmic devices to practice. Some of these devices are quite simple and others are more demanding. Each chapter is singular in and of itself and is not based on the preceding one. You can pick any chapter to begin with as they are not necessarily in an order that you must follow. Although some of the topics might appear to be quite condensed, each idea or concept is worthy of serious attention.

When working through these chapters keep in mind that the "time feel" that one uses to play a particular rhythm makes all the difference in the world. Using varied articulations and phrasings can bring a rhythm to life.

1 Notes Per Bar

The intent of this chapter is to explore various rhythmic ideas by limiting the number of notes per bar that you can play. Begin with Tune 1 *(Sleep Walk)* and improvise a solo using only three notes per bar. You can either play the same rhythm in each bar or you can try and vary the rhythm while adhering to the three-note limit.

EXAMPLE: TUNE 1

3 NOTES PER BAR WITH THE SAME RHYTHM

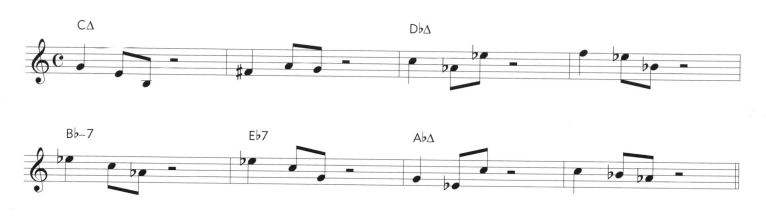

EXAMPLE: TUNE 1

3 NOTES PER BAR USING DIFFERENT RHYTHMS

Next, repeat this practice exercise using four notes per bar, five notes, six notes, and then seven notes per bar. Finally, play the exercise again using only two notes and then one note per bar. This exercise provides good ear training, that is hearing the sound of each of these steps, hearing the sound of three notes, or hearing the sound of five notes. It helps one to hear a phrase and realize the context of the line rhythmically.

EXAMPLE: TUNE 1

5 NOTES PER BAR USING DIFFERENT RHYTHMS

Needless to say, using different rhythms in every bar is more sophisticated but it is not necessarily more effective. This exercise improves your awareness of which rhythms you are using as well as your awareness of where you are in the bar. More notes per bar is not better than a few, just different.

Tune 1 ♦ *Sleep Walk* (C Instruments)

Track 3 - slow
Track 4 - fast

Track 3 - slow
Track 4 - fast

Tune 1 ◊ *Sleep Walk* (B♭ Instruments)

Track 3 - slow
Track 4 - fast

Tune 1 ◊ *Sleep Walk* (E♭ Instruments)

The next step is to try playing a specific number of notes but this time play them independent of bar lines. In other words, pick a specific number of notes and then play that grouping as many or few times as you like within a bar, over the bar, or through the bar. The following example uses three-note groupings within and over the bar lines.

EXAMPLE:

Another idea to consider is that your note groupings don't necessarily have to be connected. In this following example I am thinking of three note groupings although the listener wouldn't be able to tell that because the groupings are overlapped. The point being made here is that practicing in this way can lead you to new or different rhythmic ideas. How I'm thinking about these groupings of notes will effect the articulation of the lines.

As you can see this exercise can be as exoteric or esoteric as you like depending on your own imagination. It creates rhythms that you might not ordinarily play and it also serves as a useful tool to begin hearing polyrhythms. For example, take a five-note grouping, they could be played as simply as this:

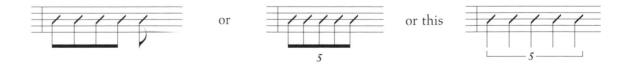

The five notes can be played as 1 beat or 1 1/2 beats, 2 beats, 3 beats, or 4 beats, etc.

2 22 Rhythms

This chapter contains 22 one-bar rhythms as well as a new tune to work with. Try playing each one-bar rhythm through Tune 2. Play each rhythm and feel it as if you were a rhythm instrument, feel the rhythm inside your body. Play through each of the 22 rhythms and get a feel for every one. Of course, add to the list! The chart is limited to primarily quarter notes and eighth notes. Sixteenth notes and triplets have been purposely omitted at this point.

22 Rhythms

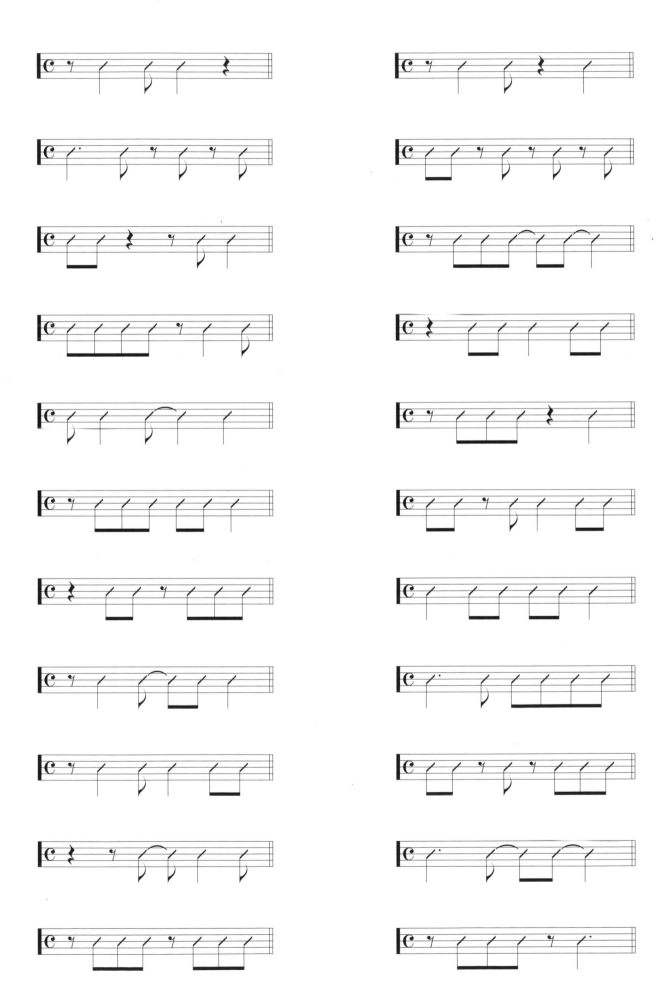

Track 5 - slow
Track 6 - fast

Tune 2 ♦ *Wine Tasting* (C Instruments)

FΔ   E♭7#11   Aø   D7alt.

G–7   B♭–Δ   E♭7#11

FΔ   D–7   G–7   C7

Eø   A7♭9   D–7   G7   G–7   C7

FΔ   E♭7#11   Aø   D7alt.

G–7   B♭–Δ   E♭7#11

FΔ   D–7   B–7   E7alt.

A–7   D–7   G–7   C7   F   D7♭9   G–7   C7

Tune 2 ◊ *Wine Tasting* (B♭ Instruments)

GΔ | F7#11 | Bø | E7alt.

A−7 | | C−Δ | F7#11

GΔ | E−7 | A−7 | D7

F#ø B7♭9 | E−7 A7 | A−7 | D7

GΔ | F7#11 | Bø | E7alt.

A−7 | | C−Δ | F7#11

GΔ | E−7 | C#−7 | F#7alt.

B−7 E−7 | A−7 D7 | G E7♭9 | A−7 D7

Tune 2 ♦ *Wine Tasting* (E♭ Instruments)

Track 5 - slow
Track 6 - fast

DΔ   C7#11   F#ø   B7alt.

E–7   G–Δ   C7#11

DΔ   B–7   E–7   A7

C#ø   F#7♭9   B–7   E7   E–7   A7

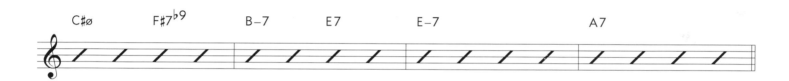

DΔ   C7#11   F#ø   B7alt.

E–7   G–Δ   C7#11

DΔ   B–7   G#–7   C#7alt.

F#–7   B–7   E–7   A7   D   B7♭9   E–7   A7

After playing each of the one-bar rhythms through Tune 2 the next step is to alter the placement of each rhythm. For example, you can play each rhythm one beat early, or two beats early, or one beat late, and so on. These following exercises will help you to hear rhythms independent of bar lines and will help you to develop "phrasing over the bar line."

Notice that by displacing a rhythm 1/2 of a beat, or 1 1/2 beats, or 2 1/2 beats, you create entirely different sounding rhythms at times.

22 Rhythms played one beat early:

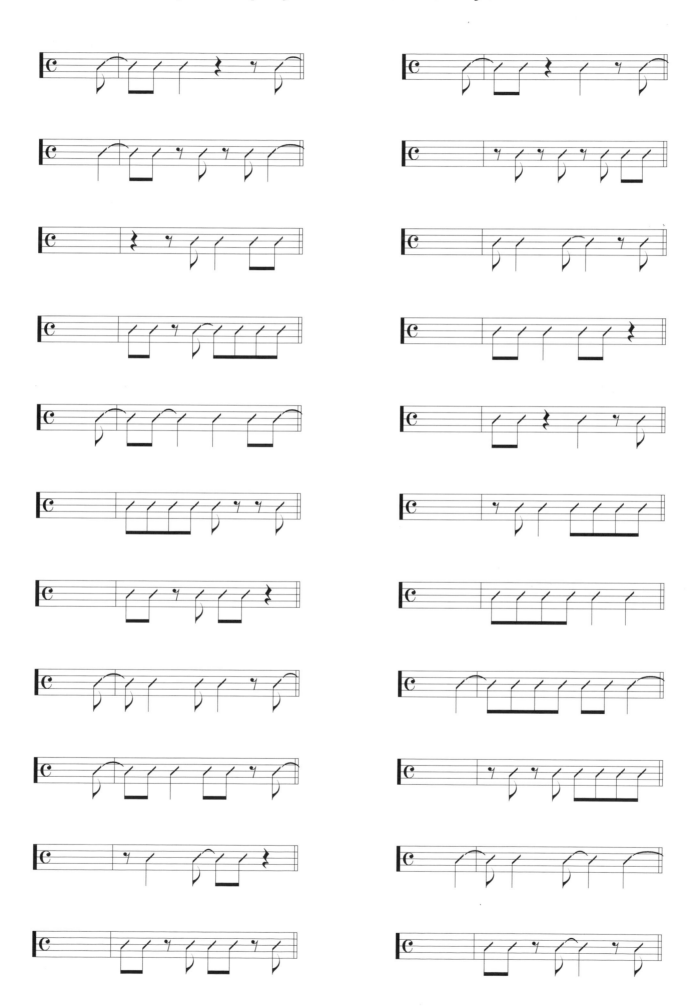

22 Rhythms played two beats early:

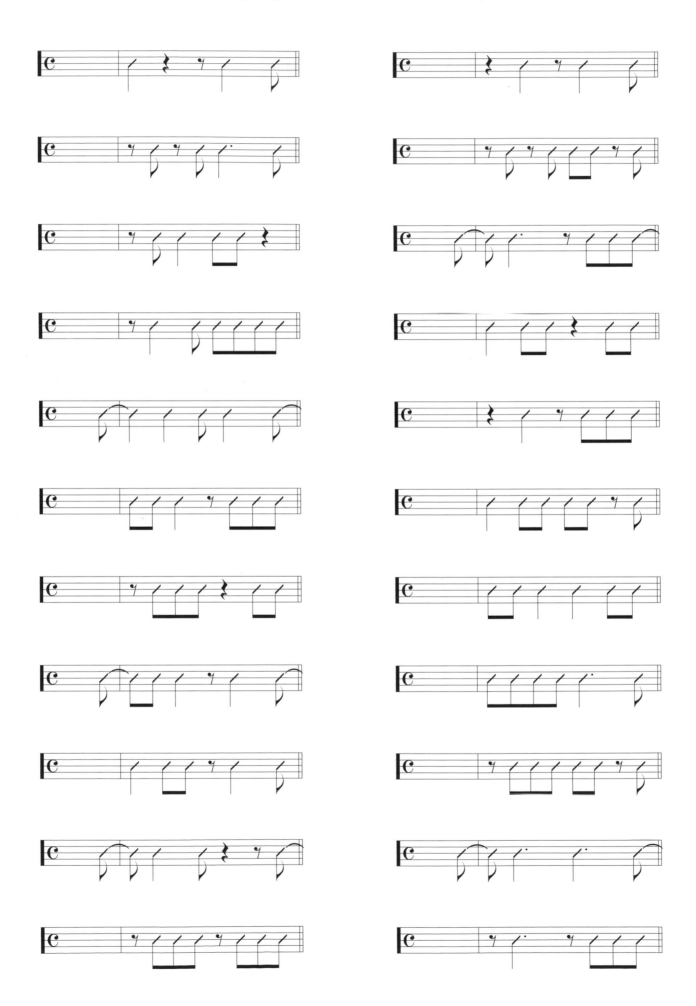

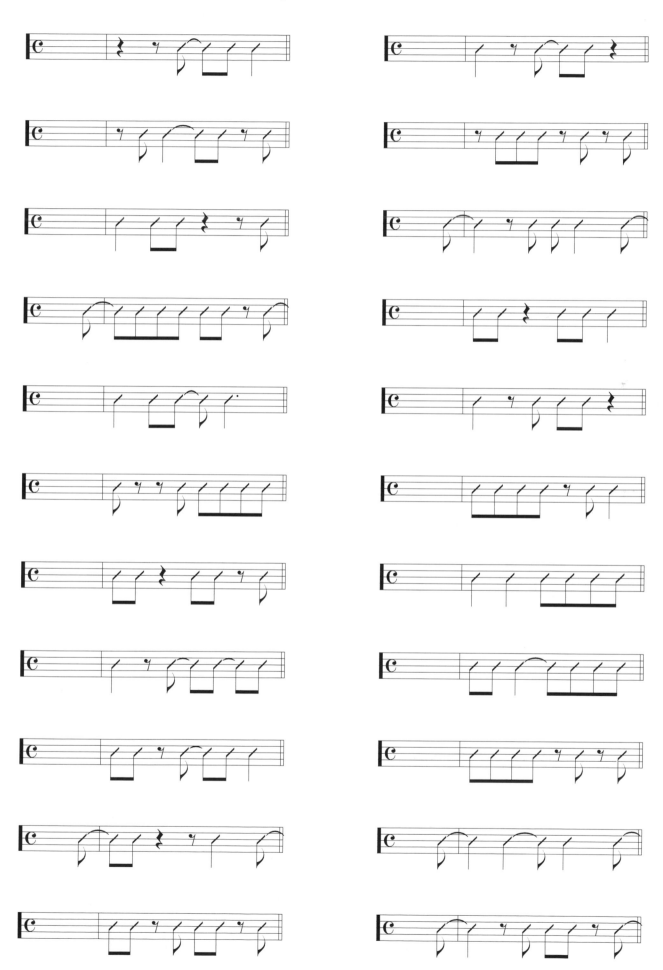

22 Rhythms played one beat delayed:
(three beats early)

22 Rhythms anticipated by a 1/2 beat:

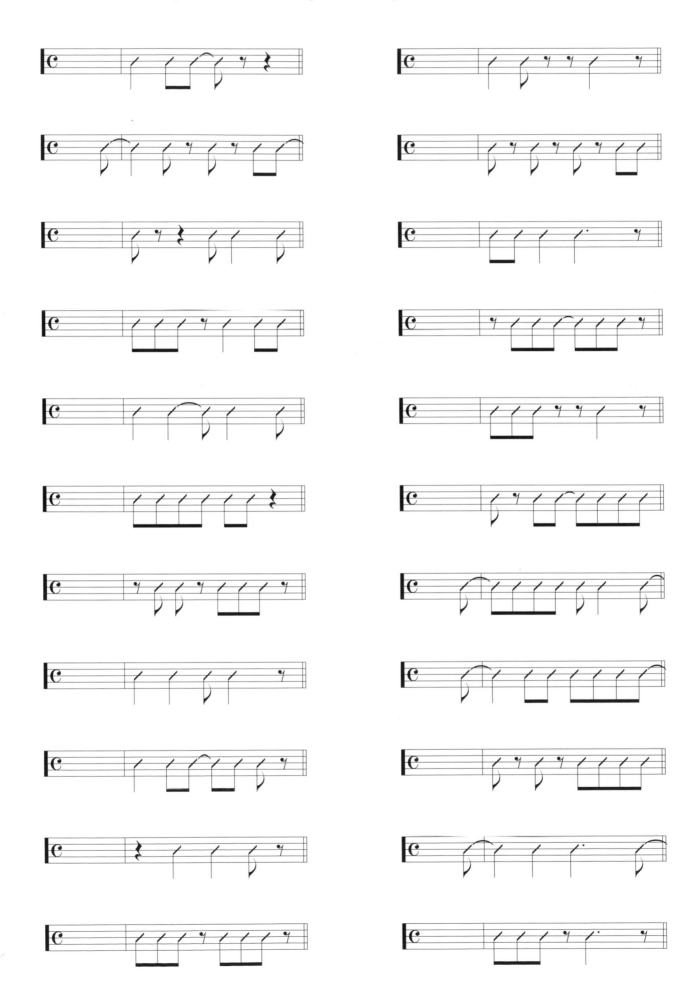

22 Rhythms anticipated by 1 1/2 beats:

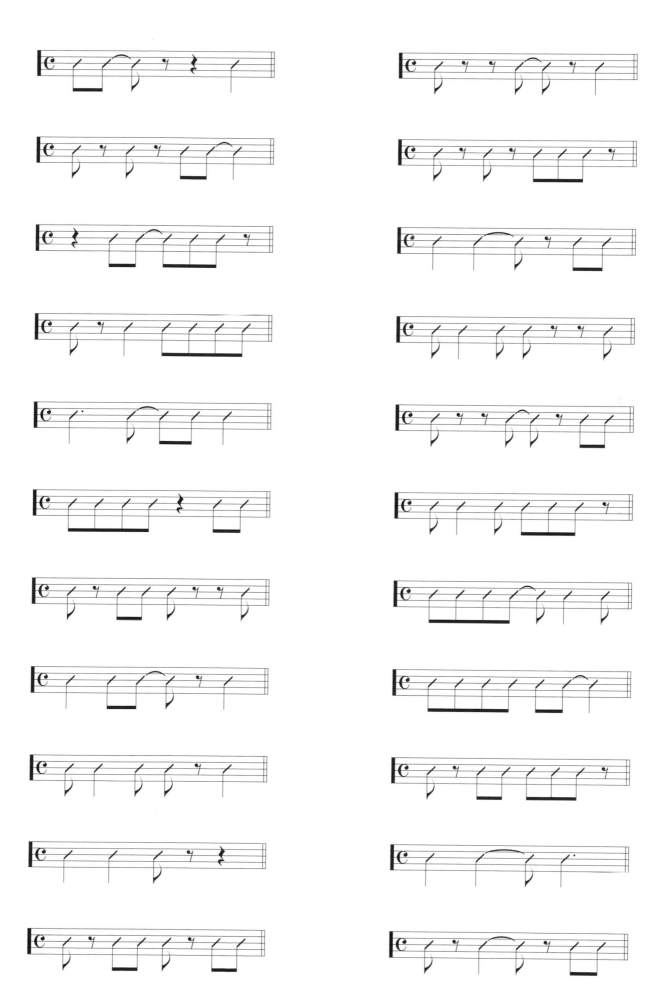

22 Rhythms anticipated by 2 1/2 beats:

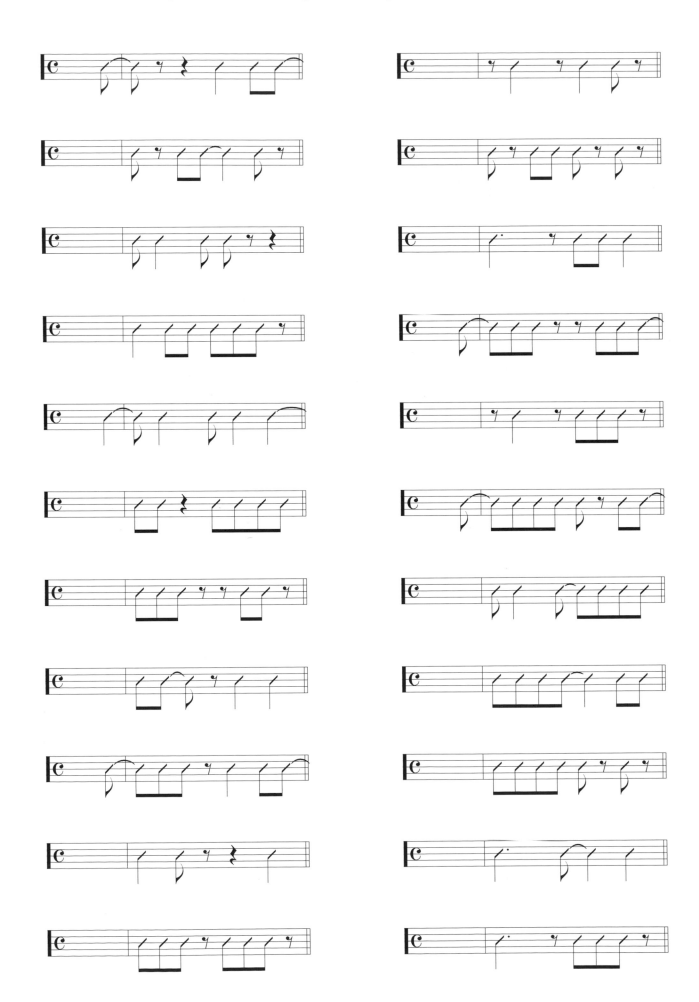

22 Rhythms delayed by a 1/2 beat:

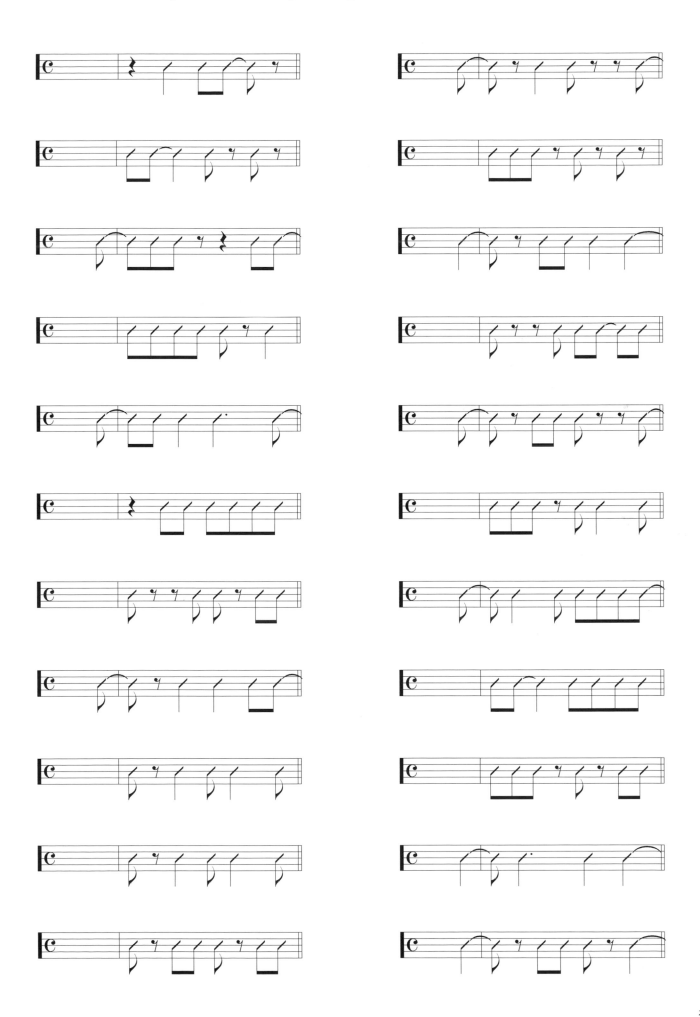

Note that many of the eighth-note downbeats might have been written as quarter notes. In these preceding pages they were written as eighth notes to keep clear the connection to the original 22 rhythms.

Having played through these various displacements of each rhythm you can now combine two of the one-bar rhythms. Create a two-bar rhythm and play it through a tune. Combine three one-bar rhythms and create a three-bar rhythm and play it through a tune. Combine four one-bar rhythms and create a four-bar rhythm and play it through a tune.

This is an example of combining rhythm 1 and 4, to make a two-bar rhythm:

3 Eighth-Note Rhythms

To begin exploring eighth-note rhythms start by playing 4 consecutive eighth notes as a one-bar rhythm. Next, displace the grouping by starting on eight different places in the bar.

Use Tunes 1, 2, and 3 to practice the following rhythmic groupings:

1. Starting on one.

2. Starting on the "and" of beat one.

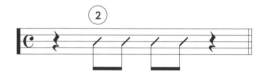

3. Starting on beat two.

4. Starting on the "and" of beat two.

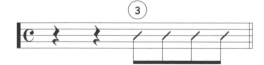

5. On this rhythm the last eighth note would sound the next chord.

For #6, #7, and #8, the harmony can be anticipated. That is, starting on the "and" of three, beat four, or the "and" of four, you can anticipate the next chord by either approaching notes of the next chord or by simply sounding the next chord.

6. Starting on the "and" of beat three.

7. Starting on beat four.

8. Starting on the "and" of beat four.

9. Try playing four consecutive eighth notes on different beats randomly, for example:

10. Next, try the following four-note grouping which will result in the superimposition of one time signature over another. This is a 3/4 pattern which takes three bars of 4/4 to work out.

11. Here's another 3/4 pattern:

12. Here's a 5/4 pattern over 4/4 and it takes five bars to work out.

13. Here is a 7/4 pattern over 4/4.

After practicing #10-13, try going back to #9 and using some of these various time signature devices. Practicing with these devices opens up a window in the part of the mind that hears bigger spaces of time and this develops form awareness. It enables you to play creative and adventurous rhythms and be fully aware of where you are in the tune.

4 Playing Five Consecutive Eighth Notes

Using Tunes 1, 2, and 3, practice playing five consecutive eighth notes beginning on these eight different beats within the bar.

1. Starting on beat 1.

2. Starting on the "and" of beat one.

3. Starting on beat two.

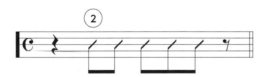

4. Starting on the "and" of beat two. The last eighth note sounds the next chord.

For #5, #6, and #7, the eighth notes before crossing the bar line can either anticipate the next chord by sounding the next chord, or they can be approach notes to the next chord, or they can sound the chord of the moment.

5. Starting on beat three.

6. Starting on the "and" of beat three.

7. Starting on the four.

8. Starting on the "and" of beat four.

9. Next, try mixing up steps 1-8. Start five consecutive eighth notes on different beats randomly, for example:

10. This is a 3/4 pattern over 4/4.

11. Here is another 3/4 pattern over 4/4 which starts on the "and" of beat one.

12. Here is a 7/4 pattern over 4/4.

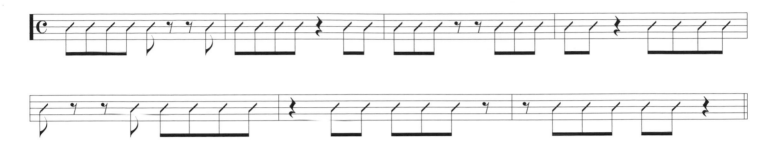

13. Here is a 9/4 pattern over 4/4.

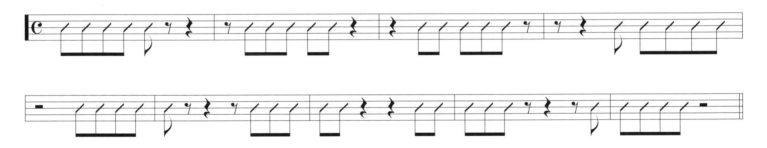

14. This is a 5/4 pattern over 4/4.

After practicing #10-14, try going back to #9 and using some of these various time signature devices. Practicing with these devices opens up a window in the part of the mind that hears bigger spaces of time and this develops form awareness. It enables you to play creative and adventurous rhythms and be fully aware of where you are in the tune.

Track 7 - slow
Track 8 - fast

Tune 3 ◊ *Together Alone* (C Instruments)

D–6⁹   Eø   A7♭9♭13   D–6⁹   Eø   A7♭9♭13

D–6⁹   Aø   D7♭9♭13   G–7

B–7   E7   G–7   C7   FΔ   E–7   A7

1.
DΔ   2.
                                          DΔ

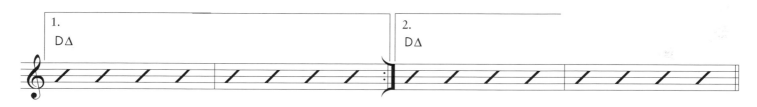

Aø   D7♭9♭13   G–

Gø   C7♭9♭13   FΔ   Eø   A7♭9♭13

D–6⁹   Eø   A7♭9♭13   D–6⁹   Eø   A7♭9♭13

D–   B7alt.   E7alt.   A7alt.   D–   Eø   A7♭9♭13

Tune 3 ◊ *Together Alone* (B♭ Instruments)

E−6⁹   F♯ø   B7♭9♭13   E−6⁹   F♯ø   B7♭9♭13

E−6⁹   Bø   E7♭9♭13   A−7

C♯−7   F♯7   A−7   D7   G△   F♯−7   B7

1.   E△   2.   E△

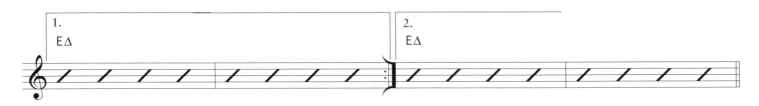

Bø   E7♭9♭13   A−

Aø   D7♭9♭13   G△   F♯ø   B7♭9♭13

E−6⁹   F♯ø   B7♭9♭13   E−6⁹   F♯ø   B7♭9♭13

E−   C♯7alt.   F♯7alt.   B7alt.   E−   F♯ø   B7♭9♭13

Track 7 - slow
Track 8 - fast

Tune 3 ♦ *Together Alone* (E♭ Instruments)

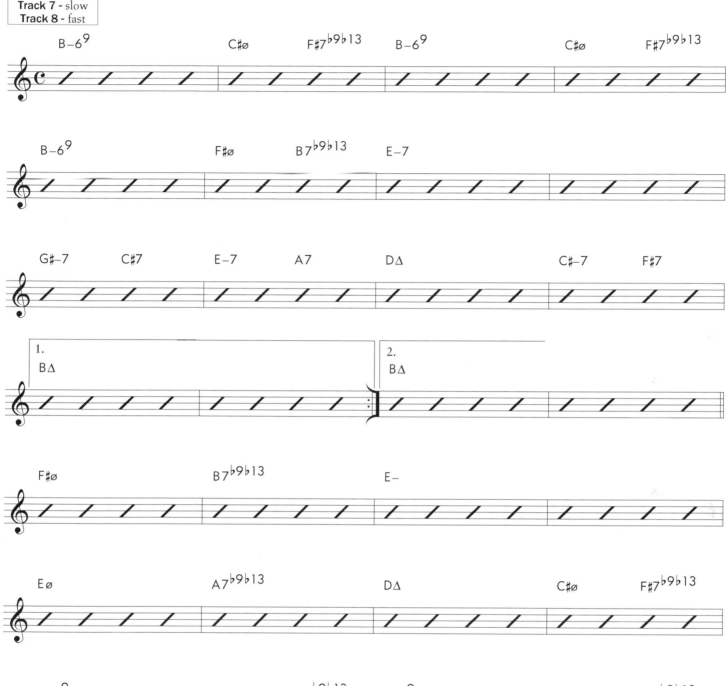

35

5 Playing Six Consecutive Eighth Notes

Using Tunes 1, 2, 3 and 4, practice playing six consecutive eighth notes starting on different places within the bar.

1. Starting on beat one.

2. Starting on the "and" of beat one.

3. Starting on beat two. The last eighth note anticipates the next chord.

4. Starting on the "and" of beat two.

When starting on beats 3, 3 "and," 4, or 4 "and," these eighth notes can anticipate the next chord, or they can be approach notes to the next chord, or they can sound the chord of the moment.

5. Starting on beat three.

6. Starting on the "and" of beat three.

7. Starting on beat four.

8. Starting on the "and" of beat four.

9. Try starting six consecutive eighth notes form different beats randomly, for example:

10. Here is 7/4 pattern over 4/4.

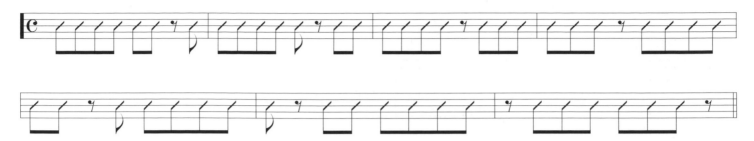

11. Here is a 9/4 pattern over 4/4.

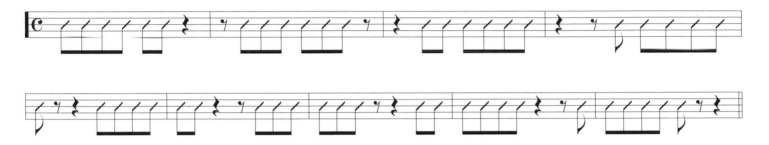

12. This is a 5/4 pattern over 4/4.

13. This is another 5/4 pattern over 4/4.

14. This is 6/4 pattern over 4/4.

After practicing #10-14 go back and try #9 again using some of these time signature devices.

Track 9 - slow
Track 10 - fast

Tune 4 ♦ *It's No One But You* (C Instruments)

G–7   C7   FΔ   D7♭9

G–7   C7   FΔ   C–7   F7

B♭–7   E♭7   A♭Δ   D♭7

CΔ   A7   D–7   G7   C   A–7   D7

G–7   C7   FΔ   D7♭9

G–7   C7   C–7   F7

B♭Δ   B♭–7   E♭7   A–7   A♭–7   D♭7

G–7   C7   FΔ   A–7   D7

Tune 4 ♦ *It's No One But You* (B♭ Instruments)

A–7   D7   GΔ   E7♭9

A–7   D7   GΔ   D–7   G7

C–7   F7   B♭Δ   E♭7

DΔ   B7   E–7   A7   D   B–7   E7

A–7   D7   GΔ   E7♭9

A–7   D7   D–7   G7

CΔ   C–7   F7   B–7   B♭–7   E♭7

A–7   D7   GΔ   B–7   E7

Track 9 - slow
Track 10 - fast

Tune 4 ♦ *It's No One But You* (E♭ Instruments)

6 Playing Seven Consecutive Eighth Notes

Using Tunes 1, 2, 3 and 4, practice playing seven consecutive eighth notes starting on different places within the bar.

1. Starting on beat one.

2. Starting on the "and" of beat one.

3. Starting on beat two.

4. Starting on the "and" of beat two.

5. Starting on beat three.

6. Starting on the "and" of beat three.

7. Starting on beat four.

8. Starting on the "and" of beat four.

9. Try starting seven consecutive eighth notes from different beats randomly, for example:

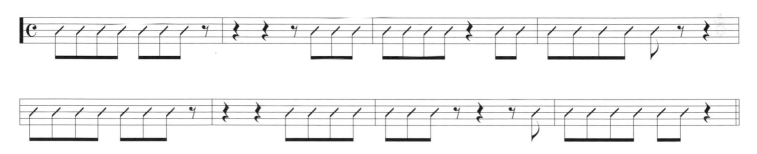

10. This is a 7/4 pattern over 4/4.

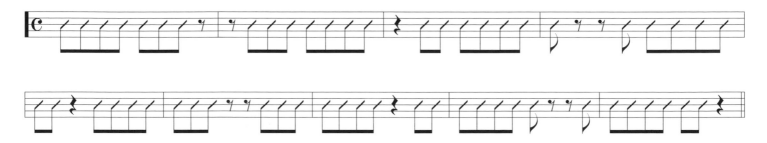

11. This is a 5/4 pattern over 4/4.

12. This is a 5/4 pattern over 4/4.

13. This is a 6/4 pattern over 4/4.

14. This is an 11/4 pattern over 4/4.

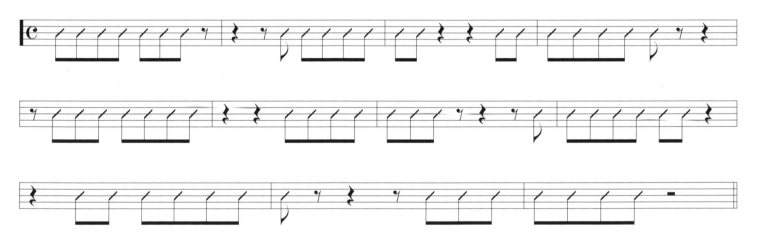

After practicing #10-14 go back and try #9 again using some of these time signature devices.

7 Playing Three Consecutive Eighth Notes

Using Tunes 1, 2, and 3, practice playing groupings of three consecutive eighth notes starting on different places within the bar.

1. Starting on beat one.

2. Starting on the "and" of beat one.

3. Starting on beat two.

4. Starting on the "and" of beat two.

5. Starting on beat three.

6. Starting on the "and" of beat three.

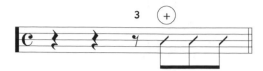

7. Starting on beat four.

8. Starting on the "and" of beat four.

9. Try starting three consecutive eighth notes from different beats randomly.

The following exercises, 10-13, are written out in varying time signatures but should be played superimposed over 4/4. Practicing these rhythms will also help you to gain familiarity with playing in these odd meters.

10. Play this 3/4 pattern over 4/4.

11. Play this 3/4 pattern over 4/4.

12. Play this 5/4 pattern over 4/4.

13. Play this 7/4 pattern over 4/4.

14. Try playing exercise #9 again using the additional rhythmic devices.

8 Playing Two Consecutive Eighth Notes

At this point having worked on the preceding chapters and gotten the gist of this exercise, try and play random groupings of two eighth notes starting at various places within the bar. Here are some rhythms to consider:

1. This is a 3/4 rhythmic pattern using two consecutive eighth notes.

2. This is a 5/4 rhythmic pattern using two consecutive eighth notes.

3. This is a 7/4 rhythmic pattern using two consecutive eighth notes.

Try playing random two's on Tunes 1, 2 and 3.

9 Triplet Groupings

Using Tune 5 *(It Happened)*, practice the following triplet rhythms. Each one consists of two groupings of eighth-note triplets, but only four of the six notes are sounded.

1.

2.

3.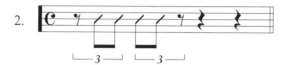

4.

5.

6.

7.

8.

9.

10.
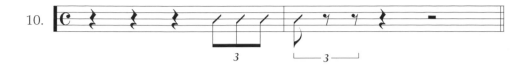

11.

12.

13.
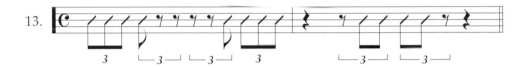

To get used to playing exercise #13, try playing the same four-note melody starting on the different beats, for example:

Now try to play the four-note melody wherever it appears in the bar with the same articulation.

14. Try this 5/4 triplet rhythm over 4/4.

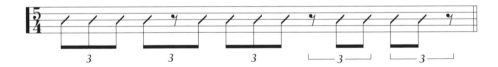

15. Try this 7/4 triplet rhythm over 4/4.

16. Practice playing these preceding triplet groupings randomly.

Tune 5 ◊ *It Happened* (C Instruments)

Eb△   E°7   F−7   F#°7

Eb△/G   Eb7   Ab△   Gø   C7^{b9b13}

F−7   Db7$^{\#11}$ Eb△   Dø   G7^{b9}

C−7   F7   F−7   Bb7

Eb△   E°7   F−7   F#°7

Eb   Eb7   Ab△   Gø   C7^{b9b13}

F−7   Db7$^{\#11}$ Eb△   C7^{b9}

F−7   Bb7   Eb   C7   F−7   Bb7

Tune 5 ♦ *It Happened* (B♭ Instruments)

F△   F#°7   G–7   G#°7

F△/A   F7   B♭△   Aø   D7♭9♭13

G–7   E♭7#11   F△   Eø   A7♭9

D–7   G7   G–7   C7

F△   F#°7   G–7   G#°7

F   F7   B♭△   Aø   D7♭9♭13

G–7   E♭7#11   F△   D7♭9

G–7   C7   F   D7   G–7   C7

Tune 5 ♦ *It Happened* (E♭ Instruments)

Track 11 - slow
Track 12 - fast

CΔ   C#°7   D–7   D#°7

CΔ/E   C7   FΔ   Eø   A7♭9♭13

D–7   B♭7#11   CΔ   Bø   E7♭9

A–7   D7   D–7   G7

CΔ   C#°7   D–7   D#°7

C   C7   FΔ   Eø   A7♭9♭13

D–7   B♭7#11   CΔ   A7♭9

D–7   G7   C   A7   D–7   G7

10 Five Consecutive Eighth-Note Triplets

Using Tune 5 *(It Happened)*, practice the following triplet rhythms. Each consists of two or three eighth-note triplet groupings but only five of the notes are sounded.

1.

2.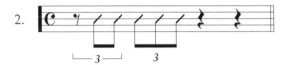

3.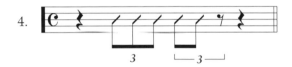

4.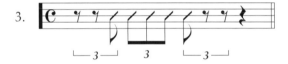

5.

6.

7.

8.

9.

10.

11.

12.

13.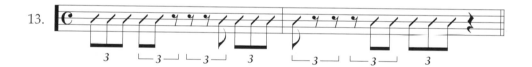

14. Try playing this 7/4 rhythm over 4/4.

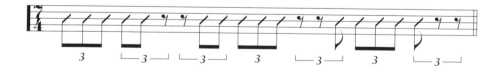

15. Practice playing five consecutive eighth-note triplets randomly.

11 Six Consecutive Eighth-Note Triplets

Using Tune 5 *(It Happened)*, practice the following triplet rhythms.

1.
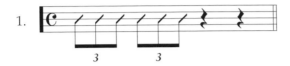

2.
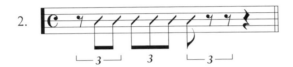

3.
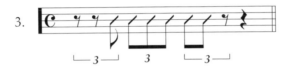

4.

5.

6.

7.

8.

9.

10.

11.

12.

13.

14. Try this 7/4 rhythm over 4/4.

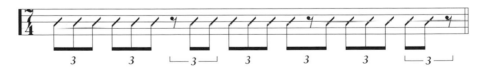

15. Practice playing six consecutive eighth-note triplets randomly.

12 Seven Consecutive Eighth-Note Triplets

Using Tune 5 *(It Happened)*, practice the following triplet rhythms.

1.
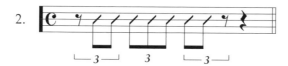

2.
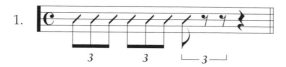

3.

4.

5.

6.
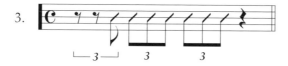

7.

8.

9.

10.

11.

12.
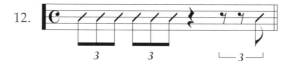

13.
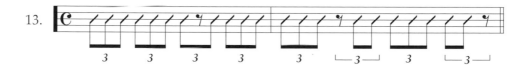

14. Try this 10/4 rhythm over 4/4.

15. Practice playing seven consecutive eighth-note triplets randomly.

13 Three Consecutive Eighth-Note Triplets

Using Tune 5 *(It Happened)*, practice the following triplet rhythms.

1.

2.

3.

4.

5.

6.

7.

8.

9.

10.

11.

12.

13.

14. Try this 5/4 rhythm over 4/4.

15. Practice playing three consecutive eighth-note triplets randomly.

16. Try playing two consecutive eighth-note triplets.

17. Try playing two consecutive eighth-note triplets randomly.

14 Mixing Up Different Groups of Consecutive Eighth Notes

REVIEW OF CHAPTERS 3-8 • CONSECUTIVE EIGHTH NOTES

To review material presented in Chapters 3-8, practice playing broken eighth-note solos using varying groupings of eighth notes as in the following example.

EXAMPLE: TUNE 5 - *It Happened*

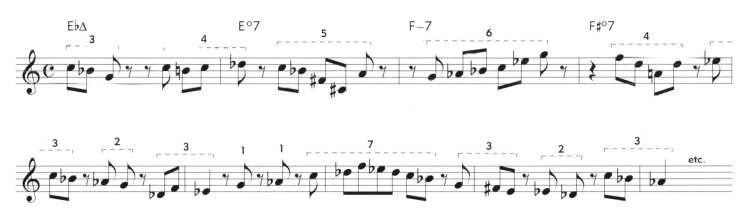

Who's counting? The seasoned improviser is not counting the number of eighth notes as he or she plays. But practicing in this way and playing these exercises does give the improviser a new awareness of what it is he or she is playing.

REVIEW OF CHAPTERS 9-13 • CONSECUTIVE TRIPLETS

To review the material pertaining to consecutive triplets in Chapters 9-13, try playing broken triplet solos on Tune 5 using a variety of triplet groupings as in the following example.

EXAMPLE: TUNE 5 - *It Happened*

15 Consecutive 16th Notes

To practice playing consecutive sixteenth notes take the material presented in Chapters 3-8 on consecutive eighth notes and convert them to sixteenth-note exercises by doubling up. For example, (the first rhythm of Chapter 3) four consecutive eighth notes and two quarter-note rests, becomes four consecutive sixteenth-notes and one quarter-note rest.

The exercises are then all in 2/4 time so you can repeat the 2/4 phrase twice to make a 4/4 bar.

EXAMPLE:

EXAMPLE: 4 CONSECUTIVE NOTES

EXAMPLE: 5 CONSECUTIVE NOTES

EXAMPLE: 6 CONSECUTIVE NOTES

This way of practicing sixteenth notes is very valuable for double-time playing. It helps the improviser to actually create when playing sixteenth notes rather than being limited to a few pet phrases. Playing consecutive groups of five, six, or seven sixteenth notes is very close to playing long double-time lines. Broken sixteenth-note lines are also very effective. All of these rhythms depend a great deal on the tempo of the tune.

16 Hemiolas

This chapter presents 3/4 rhythms to be played over 4/4 tunes. Practicing this rhythmic technique helps the improviser to become independent of bar lines and makes one's playing more horizontal. Playing 3/4 rhythms over 4/4 tunes insures that the player is beginning phrases from various beats within the bar and not starting every line on only beat one. Practicing this technique opens a window in the mind that hears bigger spaces of time, like four-bar phrases or eight-bar phrases, or sixteen bars. It also effects the improviser's melodic choices because you are sometimes anticipating the next chord.

Once you've practiced these rhythms you will notice a greater sense of form control even when you aren't playing them. Try to practice these rhythms with a play along and also without a play along while your right foot taps beat one and your left foot taps beat 3. Also, try singing the rhythms to coordinate where beat one is in relation to the rhythm.

In the following chart the 3/4 rhythm is shown and then written out over a 4/4 time signature. It takes four bars of 3/4 to equal three bars of 4/4. The 3/4 rhythm starts again on the first beat after it has been played through three bars of 4/4.

Try playing these rhythms on Tune 6 *(Into Somewhere)*.

3/4 RHYTHM   WRITTEN OVER 4/4

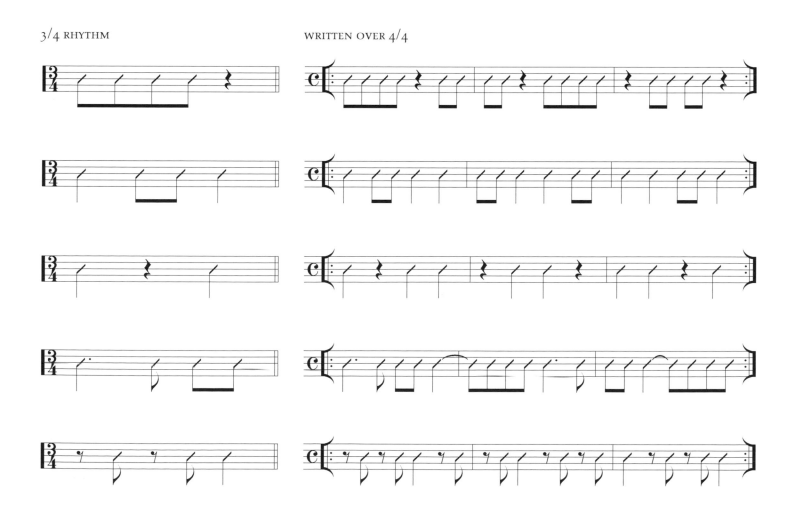

or

Track 13 - slow
Track 14 - fast

Tune 6 ♦ *Into Somewhere* (C Instruments)

GΔ   Bb–7   Eb7

GΔ   B–7   E7b9

A–   Bø   E7b9   A–7

Eb7#11   A–7   D7b9

GΔ   Bb–7   Eb7

GΔ   B–7   E7b9

A–7   Bø   E7b9   A–7   F7#11

B–7   E7   A–7   D7   GΔ   A–7   D7

Tune 6 ◊ *Into Somewhere* (B♭ Instruments)

Track 13 - slow
Track 14 - fast

Tune 6 ◆ *Into Somewhere* (E♭ Instruments)

E∆   G–7   C7

E∆   G#–7   C#7♭9

F#–   G#ø   C#7♭9   F#–7

C7#11   F#–7   B7♭9

E∆   G–7   C7

E∆   G#–7   C#7♭9

F#–7   G#ø   C#7♭9   F#–7   D7#11

G#–7   C#7   F#–7   B7   E∆   F#–7   B7

After trying these rhythms on Tune 6 go back and try playing them through Tunes 1-5. When you have become comfortable using these rhythms exclusively without stopping try combining any two of them to make a 6/4 rhythm. Here is an example:

Try combining four of them to create a line with 3/4 phrasing over 4/4 that is less obvious, for example:

Needless to say this becomes inexhaustible. You might try using different combinations every day. Once you have gone through the exercises in this chapter try just playing random 3/4 over 4/4 using one 3/4 rhythm, then another and another without any program in mind. This really gets it into your unconscious mind. You could also try composing some 3/4 rhythms and making them your own.

17 5/4 Rhythms Over 4/4

In the same fashion that you played 3/4 over 4/4 (Chapter 16) try 5/4 over 4/4. It takes five bars of 4/4 to equal four bars of 5/4. To check yourself out when practicing these rhythms the pattern should hit one on the sixth bar.

5/4 RHYTHMS

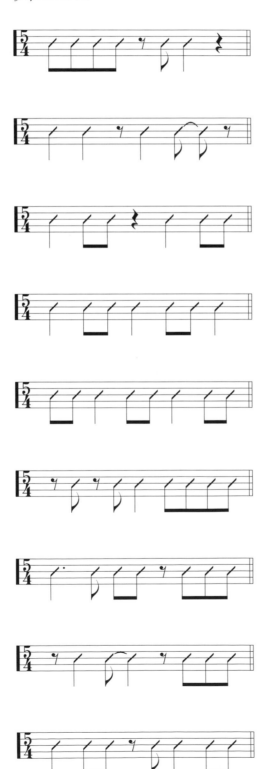

Here is that first 5/4 rhythm written out over 4/4. Try writing the rhythms out like this if it helps.
Be patient with yourself as it can take years to work this material out!

18 7/4 Rhythms Over 4/4

As with the 3/4 and 5/4 rhythms try these 7/4 rhythms over 4/4. When playing a 7/4 rhythm it takes seven bars to work out so that on the eighth bar you are starting on beat one again.

7/4 Rhythms

By starting the same rhythm on beat 2 "and" that was started on beat 1, you get a 5/4 mirror rhythm. By starting the same rhythm on beat 3 "and" as beat 1, you get a 7/4 mirror rhythm.

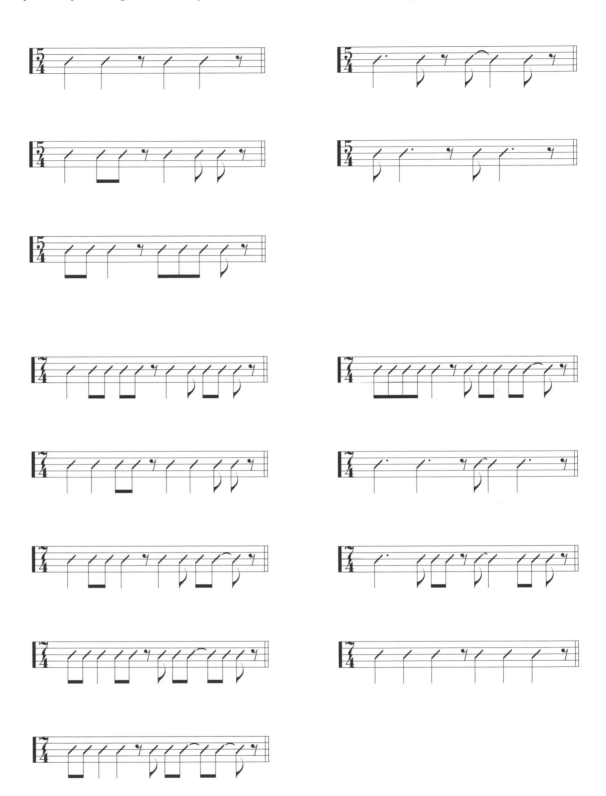

RETROGRATE MIRROR RHYTHMS

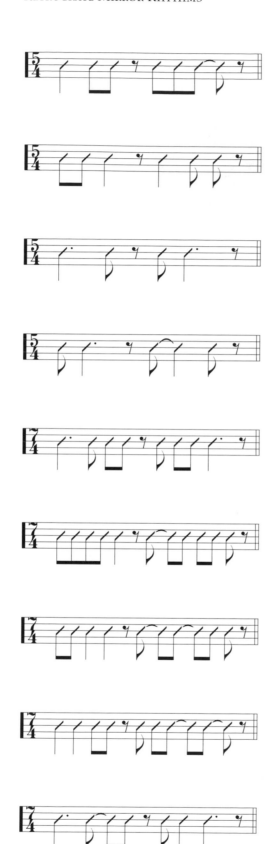

19 4/4 Rhythms Over 3/4

Take any of the 22 one-bar rhythms in Chapter 2 and play them over this 3/4 tune. Next, try combining two of those 4/4 rhythms and play them over this tune.

Tune 7 ♦ *Come and Gone* (C Instruments)

Track 15 - slow
Track 16 - fast

Track 15 - slow
Track 16 - fast

Tune 7 ◊ *Come and Gone* (B♭ Instruments)

| CΔ | E7alt. | FΔ | A7♭9♭13 |

| D−7 | A7alt. | D−7 | G7 |

| CΔ | F#ø B7♭9 | D−7 | G7 |

| CΔ | F#ø B7♭9 | D−7 | G7 |

| CΔ | E7alt. | FΔ | A7♭9♭13 |

| D−7 | A7alt. | D−7 | G7 |

| CΔ | G−7 C7 | FΔ | F#°7 |

| E−7 A7 | D−7 G7 | CΔ A7 | D−7 G7 |

Tune 7 ♦ *Come and Gone* (E♭ Instruments)

Track 15 - slow
Track 16 - fast

G△   B7alt.   C△   E7♭9♭13

A–7   E7alt.   A–7   D7

G△   C#ø   F#7♭9   A–7   D7

G△   C#ø   F#7♭9   A–7   D7

G△   B7alt.   C△   E7♭9♭13

A–7   E7alt.   A–7   D7

G△   D–7   G7   C△   C#°7

B–7   E7   A–7   D7   G△   E7   A–7   D7

20 In the Pocket

One way to improve your feel or placement of eighth notes is to notice how your eighth notes fit with the rhythm section which is often playing off of the triplet. In jazz playing, feeling the triplet can help you to feel the groove of the rhythm section and help you to place your eighth notes "in the pocket." This doesn't mean that your eighth notes should be played as triplets like in this example, but rather that your eighth notes should be able to coexist with the triplet feel behind them. Sometimes this means laying back on the eighth notes or putting some type of lob on the notes.

Practicing playing triplets is one way to get more connected to the rhythm section groove and so it can help to improve your placement of eighth notes. Try playing these triplet rhythms on Tune 8 *(One Heart)* and then play eighth notes to see if you feel a different pocket.

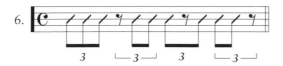

8.

9.

10.

11.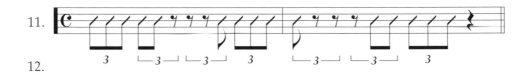

12.

Try this 7/4 rhythm over a 4/4 tune.

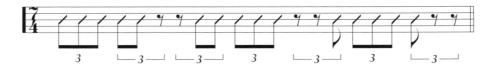

Tune 8 ◊ *One Heart* (C Instruments)

Track 17 - slow
Track 18 - fast

Bø   E7♭9   A−7   D7

G−7   C7   FΔ

Bø   E7♭9   A−7   D7

D−7   G7   G−7   C7

Aø   D7♭9♭13   G−7

B♭−7   E♭7   FΔ

Bø   E7♭9♭13   A−7   D7

G−7   C7   FΔ   D7   G−7   C7

Tune 8 ◊ *One Heart* (B♭ Instruments)

Track 17 - slow
Track 18 - fast

Tune 8 ♦ *One Heart* (E♭ Instruments)

G#ø | C#7♭9 | F#–7 | B7

E–7 | A7 | DΔ

G#ø | C#7♭9 | F#–7 | B7

B–7 | E7 | E–7 | A7

F#ø | B7♭9♭13 | E–7

G–7 | C7 | DΔ

G#ø | C#7♭9♭13 | F#–7 | B7

E–7 | A7 | DΔ B7 | E–7 A7

21 Half-Time Quarter-Note Triplet Feel

Practicing these following rhythms has the same intent as the preceding chapter, the difference being that these rhythms are twice as long as the ones in Chapter 20.

1.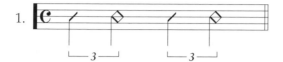

2.

3.

4.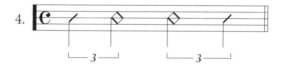

5.

6.

7.

8.

9.

10.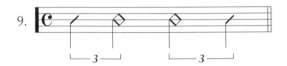

11.

12.

22 Time Zones (Polyrhythms)

One way to approach varying time zones is to talk about the different gears that might fit into the tempo at large. In this chapter we will consider five different time zones or gears to play in. It's something like driving a five-speed car.

- The quarter-note triplet gear
- The eighth-note gear
- The triplet gear
- The sixteenth-note gear
- The sextuplet gear (sixteenth-note triplets)

The aim of this chapter is to expand your vocabulary by adapting lines to these varying time zones or gears. Here is a common II–7 - V7 line:

In this line there are eight notes per measure or 16 notes in all. To make this line feel comfortable in triplet gear you need to leave off the first four or the last four notes. In this case we'll leave off the last four. Set your metronome between 50 and 60 for the half note and play the line in its original form. While playing the line as eighth notes take notice of your articulations and accents. Next play it in triplets, leaving off the last four notes.

Continue repeating the line until you are in the groove of triplets and phrasing them as if they were eighth notes.

Next try playing the line as quarter-note triplets. Again repeat the line over and over until you feel that groove.

Play it as sixteenth notes using the whole line.

If possible try playing the line as sextuplets.

Try playing this line moving from one gear to another.

To become very fluid at this try changing from one gear to another in the middle of the line, for example:

Rather than practicing this in a programmed fashion try using this technique randomly and spontaneously. In other words, don't predetermine where or how you are going to change gears but do use the same line. This practice will improve your ability to change gears using different lines. Here is another II–7 - V7 line to practice:

The above line in five gears:

1.

2.

For triplets try leaving off the first four notes.

3.

4.

5.

Try composing your own lines and adapting them to varying time zones. These lines do not have to be over particular chords or scales. You can practice this with any melody that you like the sound of without harmonic implications.

Next, take any eighth-note scale sequences or intervallic sequences that you play and practice them as triplets. Here are some examples:

SCALE SEQUENCE:

IN TRIPLETS:

SCALE SEQUENCE:

IN TRIPLETS:

INTERVALLIC SEQUENCE:

IN TRIPLETS:

Compose many other scale and intervallic sequences to really get the hang of it. Practice playing some of these time zones on Tune 9 *(Twinkle Twinkle)*. First go through the whole play-along track and try sticking to one time zone. Master that one and then go through and master the next, etc. Then try varying the zones moving from one gear to another.

Track 19 - slow
Track 20 - fast

Tune 9 ◊ *Twinkle Twinkle* (C Instruments)

Track 19 - slow
Track 20 - fast

Tune 9 ◊ *Twinkle Twinkle* (B♭ Instruments)

FΔ   G–7   C7   FΔ   F–7   B♭7

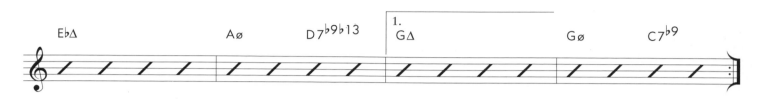

E♭Δ   A⌀   D7♭9♭13   1. GΔ   G⌀   C7♭9

2. GΔ   G⌀   C7♭9   F7   B♭Δ

B♭–7   E♭7   A♭Δ

G–7   C7   FΔ   G–7   C7

F   F–7   B♭7   E♭Δ   A⌀   D7♭9

GΔ   G⌀   C7♭9   FΔ   E7   E♭7   D7

G–7   C7   FΔ

Tune 9 ♦ *Twinkle Twinkle* (E♭ Instruments)

Track 19 - slow
Track 20 - fast

CΔ   D–7   G7   CΔ   C–7   F7

B♭Δ   E∅   A7♭9♭13   1. DΔ   D∅   G7♭9

2. DΔ   D∅   G7♭9   C7   FΔ

F–7   B♭7   E♭Δ

D–7   G7   CΔ   D–7   G7

C   C–7   F7   B♭Δ   E∅   A7♭9

DΔ   D∅   G7♭9   CΔ   B7   B♭7   A7

D–7   G7   CΔ

23 More Time Zones

This chapter is basically an extension of Chapter 22 as it considers some more advanced time gears based on 5, 7, and 9 notes per bar. Let's take the same melody we've been using and adapt it to the following time zones. Here's the melody:

Play this line or a line of your choice over and over again until you can feel the 5 against 4. Try using different articulations to enhance the sound of the line.

Five notes per bar

Five notes per bar

Quarter-note triplets (six notes per bar)

This line could also be offset by an eighth-note triplet like so:

Seven notes per bar

EIGHTH NOTES (EIGHT NOTES PER BAR)

Add one note to each bar of eighth notes or simply add two notes at the end of the original line to make nine notes per bar.

NINE NOTES PER BAR

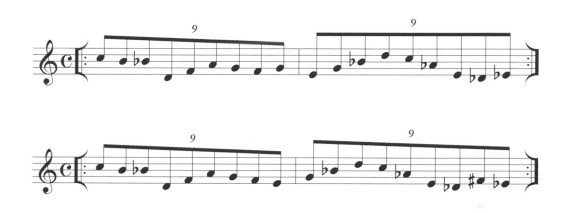

Subtract six notes from the original line to make the ten notes.

QUINTUPLETS (TEN NOTES PER BAR)

Subtract four notes from the original line.

TRIPLETS (12 NOTES PER BAR)

Subtract two notes from the original line.

SEVEN NOTES PER TWO BEATS (14 NOTES PER BAR)

SIXTEENTH NOTES (16 NOTES PER BAR)

NINE NOTES PER TWO BEATS (18 NOTES PER BAR)

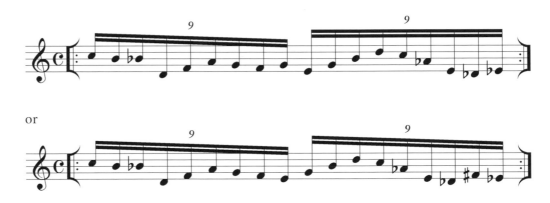

or

FIVE NOTES FOR EVERY BEAT (20 NOTES PER BAR)

or, with the addition of four notes:

SEXTUPLETS (24 NOTES PER BAR)

To continue getting into the polyrhythm mode try composing several other lines and adapting them with the above 12 gears. Also, try playing the line in repeat mode while slowing down or speeding up and keeping the original tempo in your mind. If nothing more these exercises will help to make your time more elastic and fluid and will give playing eighth notes a different perspective.

Another way to achieve similar results is to try playing scale sequences in 5, 7, or 9. Here are some examples.

This is a four-notes scale sequence played in 5/2:

Here are some five-note sequences:

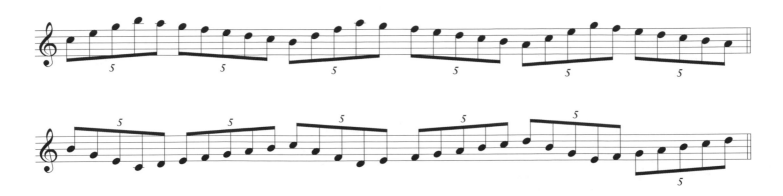

Compose some other five-note sequences.

Here are four-note sequences played in 7/2.

Seven-note sequences

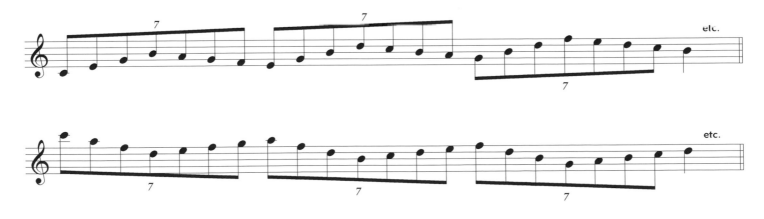

Nine-note sequences (played over four beats or two beats depending on the tempo).

Compose your own sequences and get inside the polyrhythmic gears. Once you get the feel of a particular gear try to improvise on or against tunes. Sometimes it can definitely feel as if you are playing against the tune if the rhythm section is already playing other cross rhythms or poly-rhythms. Practicing all of these lines and sequences is meant to help develop rhythmic ear training as opposed to adding melodic vocabulary.

Another way to practice rhythmic ear training is to try playing the modes in different groupings. Here are the modes written out in quintuplets, play each one twice. Note that as you play through the modes you are changing one note every time you change modes. Go through all of the modes changing one note until you finally change the root and then start all over again!

MODES IN QUINTUPLETS

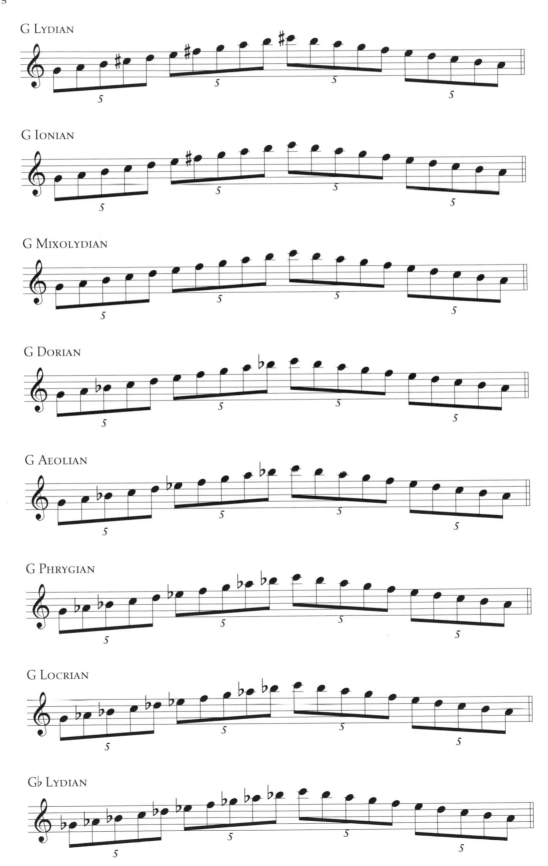

Next try the modes in septuplets.

MODES IN SEPTUPLETS

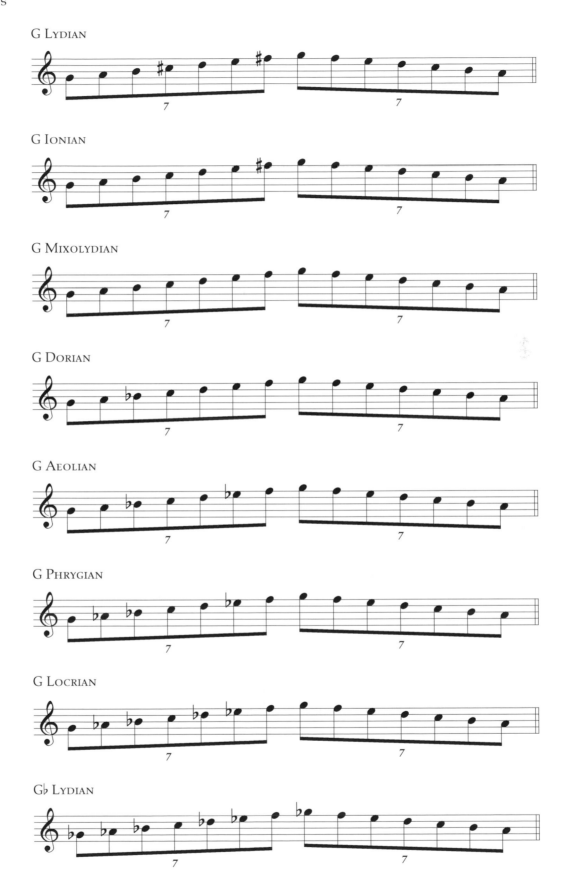

MODES IN NONTUPLETS

G LYDIAN

G IONIAN

G MIXOLYDIAN

G DORIAN

G AEOLIAN

G PHRYGIAN

G LOCRIAN

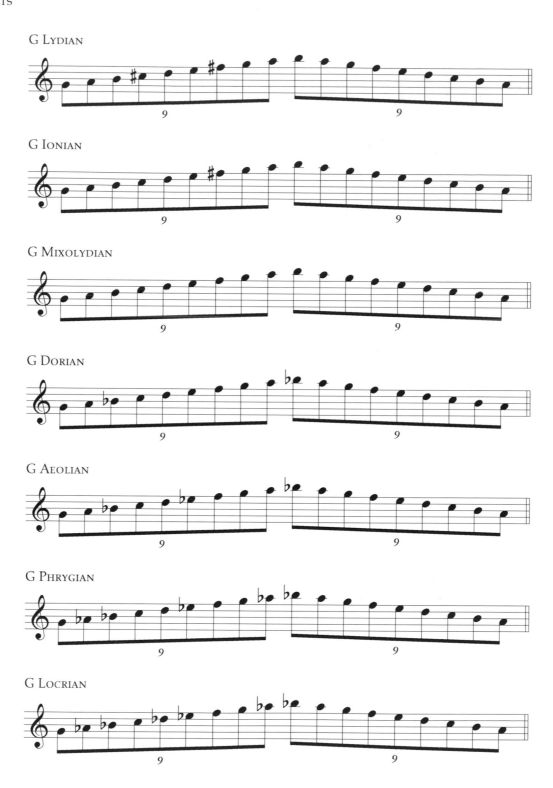

Begin again with G♭ Lydian.

Becoming adept at playing all of these polyrhythms isn't a weekly pursuit but rather a long range endeavour!

MODES IN TRIPLETS

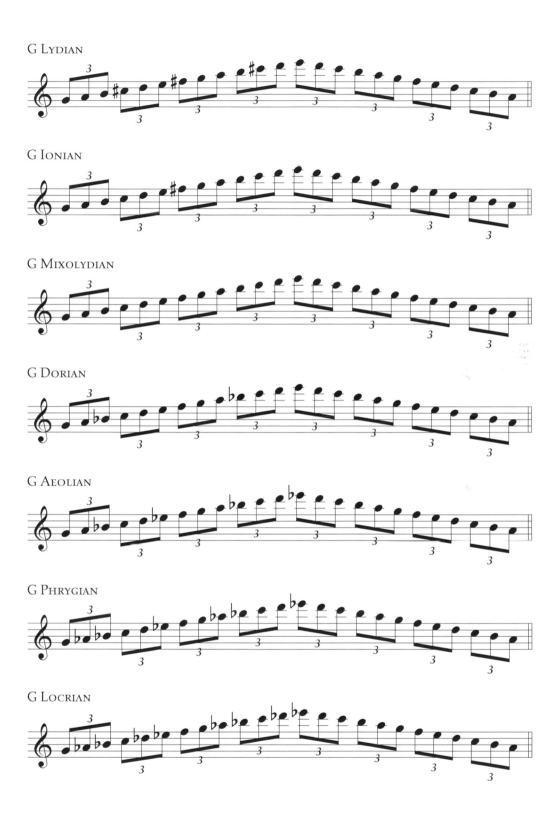

Begin again with G♭ Lydian.

24 Broken Quintuplets, Septuplets, and Nonuplets

Using any of the preceding tunes next practice some varying time zones and see if you can incorporate some broken quintuplets, septuplets, or nonuplets.

Examples of broken quintuplets: Try these over 4/4.

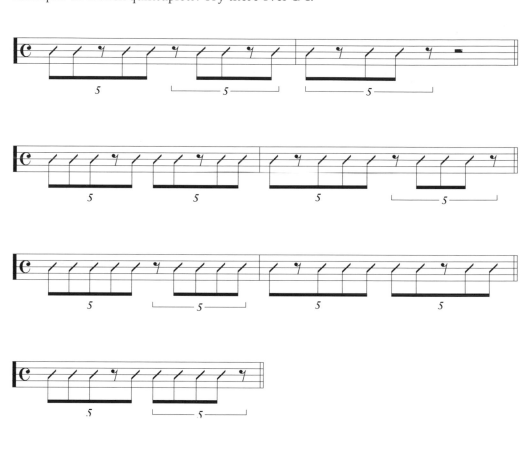

Compose some other broken quintuplet rhythms and play them on a tune. Also, these rhythms could be 5 over 4, or 5 over 3.

Examples of broken septuplets:

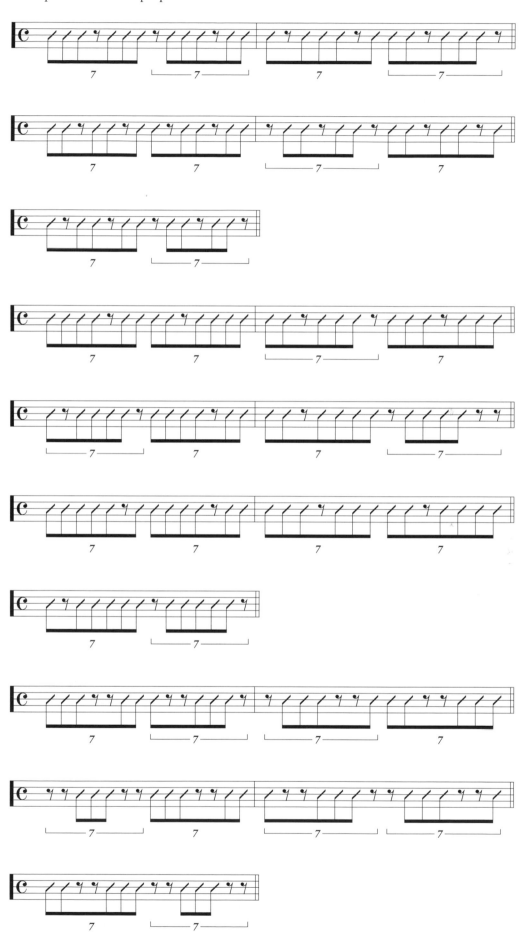

As with the quintuplets, compose some other broken septuplet rhythms and practice them over tunes. You can try those septuplet rhythms over four beats, three beats, or two beats.

Examples of broken nonuplets:

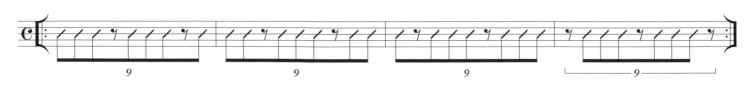

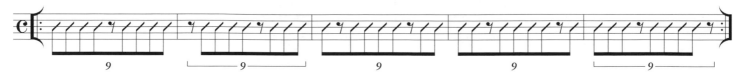

Compose other broken nonuplets and play them over two, three, or four beats.

25 Switching Gears

The intent of the exercises presented in this chapter is again rhythmic ear training. Practicing "switching gears" is meant to develop the ability to change from one polyrhythm to another in an effortless way. One could write an entire book on each one of these chapters. The exercises presented here and throughout this book are just a few suggestions of the many possibilities that can be used. By all means compose more exercises and make them your own!

Try playing these next exercises first using any notes, then maybe just notes from one chord, and then finally over the tunes. Each rhythm is written out in a repeat format so you can get used to changing back and forth between the different time zones.

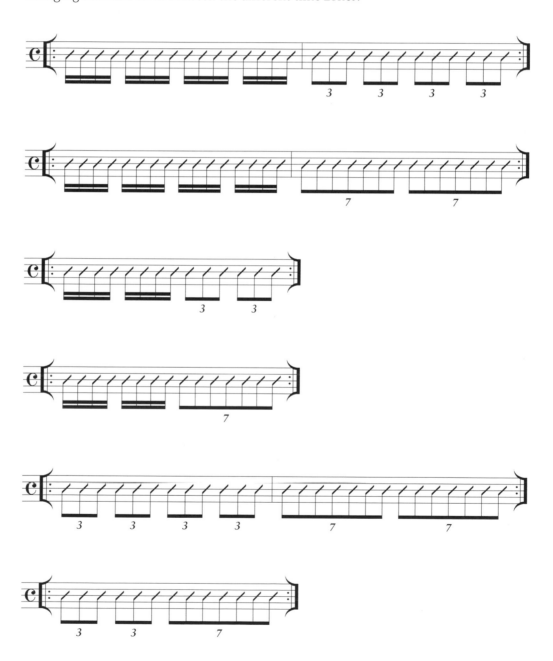

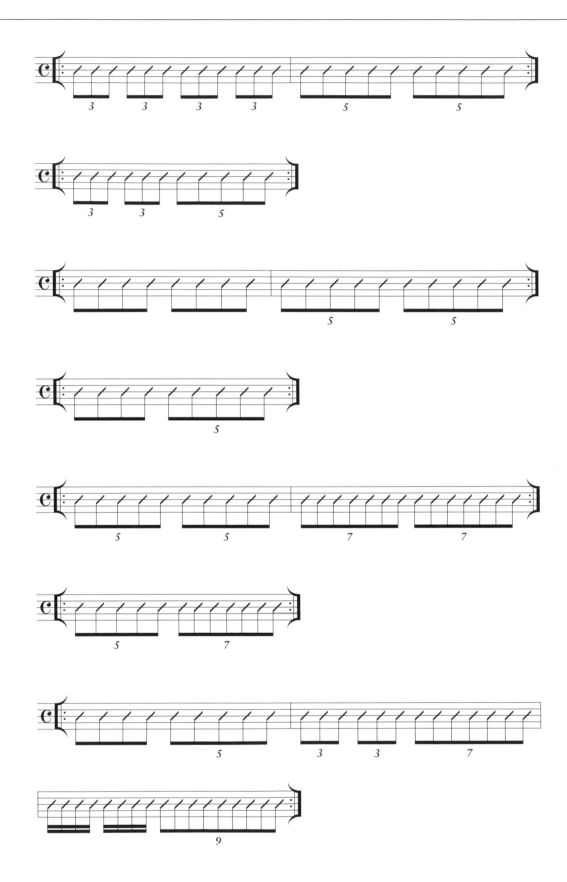

If you need another challenge try moving all of the exercises over and starting them one beat early, or try one beat late, so that the polyrhythm goes over the 4/4 bar line. Try randomly changing from one gear to another. To achieve a natural and fluid feeling while playing these changing gears can take years of practice. Just trying it however gives you another perspective on time.

26 Contraction and Expansion

Take a group of notes and try playing them over two beats. For example try this five-note grouping:

Expand and try playing these five notes over three beats, and then over four beats. Next try playing the same five notes over 1 1/2 beats by contracting them.

Try taking a three-note melody like,

and play it in one beat, then two beats, three beats, and four beats. Try playing the notes in 1 1/2 beats, or play these notes three times in two beats like so:

This concept of expansion or contraction is another way to perceive odd groupings of notes. Try this technique on any of the tunes.

27 Downbeat - Upbeat
(Quarter-Note Playing)

Here is another conceptual approach to consider. Try playing just downbeats. Play many in succession as broken downbeats. Playing this way really states a commitment as to where the soloist is perceiving the time. Next try to play just upbeats. Play an entire solo using only upbeats. Listen to your favorite players and notice the way in which they play quarter notes as downbeats and upbeats.

Mix up downbeats and upbeats on this next tune.

Track 21 - slow
Track 22 - fast

Tune 10 ♦ *There Is Another You* (C Instruments)

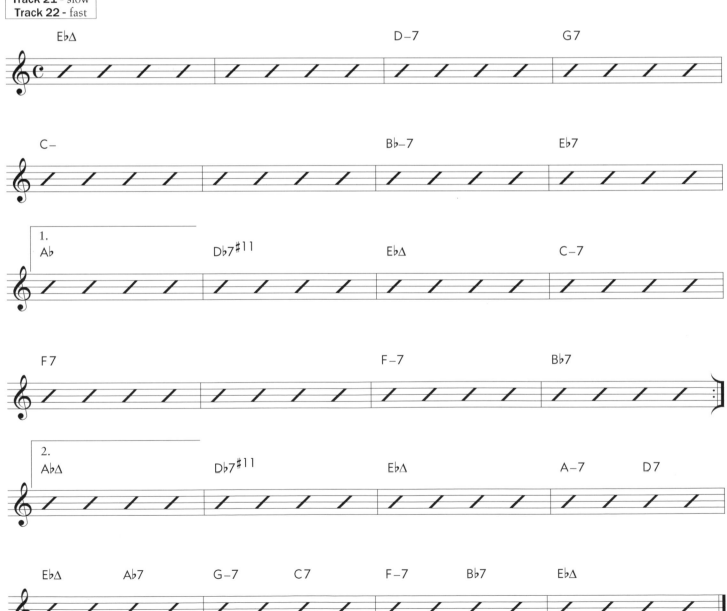

Tune 10 ♦ *There Is Another You* (B♭ Instruments)

F△   E–7   A7

D–   C–7   F7

1.
B♭   E♭7#11   F△   D–7

G7   G–7   C7

2.
B♭△   E♭7#11   F△   B–7   E7

F△   B♭7   A–7   D7   G–7   C7   F△

Track 21 - slow
Track 22 - fast

Tune 10 ♪ *There Is Another You* (E♭ Instruments)

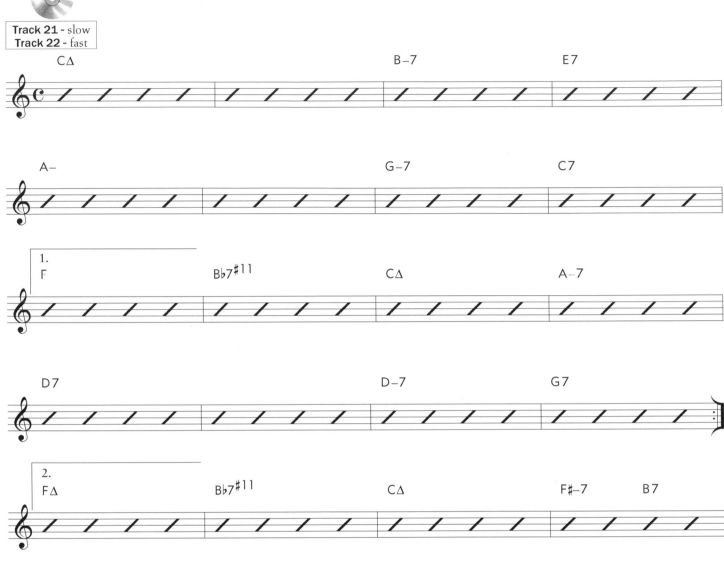

28 The Half Note, Quarter Note, and Dotted Quarter

Very often, less is more. Playing less notes at times allows the music to breath more. It also gives the rhythm section space for a little interaction and dialogue. Try playing solos on any of the tunes using only half notes, quarter notes, and dotted quarters. How rigidly you interpret this is entirely up to you. Sometimes a little limitation can be a great teacher.

29 Accents

Very often players ask: "How do I connect with the rhythm section?" I can remember hearing a really swinging trombone player and when I asked him about his approach his answer was, "I play accents and the fills around them."

Try taking any tune and playing just accents as if you were the saxophone or trumpet section in a big band. After playing through several choruses, slowly fill in around the accents.

30 Feeling the Music in 1, 2, or 4

To enhance your flexibility with the time it is great practice to play tunes with different time feelings in mind. Play a tune first thinking and feeling the tune in four, feel and think four beats to the measure. Next play that tune in two, feeling and thinking of the tune in half time (feeling beats one and three). Notice that your ideas seem to take a different shape and that your feeling of the tune can be more relaxed.

Fast tempo tunes are easier to play when you are feeling the tune in two. Sometimes to get a more lyrical feel on a tune, or even a ballad feel you can think in one, one beat per measure. If the tune is around 400, of course thinking in one is easier.

Players often seem to feel more free when playing ballads. They are able to play slow, or fast, play across the time or change time zones. This is more difficult to do when the tune is medium or medium up and the band is walking in four. Sometimes the soloist seems to be trapped in playing all eighth notes. (All eighth notes isn't necessarily bad, the right player makes it sound like the right thing to do.) But if you want to get out of that zone for contrast try feeling the music in two or one. Try even perceiving a fast tune as a ballad.

31 The Metronome

Some people say that it is best to practice with a metronome and others are dead against it. I feel that the metronome is a useful tool in that it can keep you honest. The metronome doesn't lie. On the other hand, it can also make you dependent on an outside click rather than on your own internalized time. It's good to be able to play with or without one. Time is not metronomic so one needs to learn to be flexible.

Try playing in back of the time or on top of the time. Try using the metronome on 2 and 4, or 1 and 3, or just 3, or just 4, or on the and of 2 and 4:

Also, practice without using a metronome. Internalize the rhythm section. Try to meditate on a tempo. Pick a tempo and try to just hear quarter notes, then add triplets or whatever the appropriate rhythms are that you want to hear. Notice that when you become tranquil inside you then have a better perception of the time. Relax, above all, relax!

32 Rhythmizing Scale Sequences

Below are several scale or modal sequences to work with. Some are repeated but written as descending rather than ascending. You can use these or any of your own for the next exercises.

SCALE SEQUENCES

First play the pattern starting from every degree of the scale (in other words modally transposing it). In the example below all of the notes are played over a dominant sus 4 chord. This allows you to hear the sound of the key without having to deal with any avoid notes.

(You can also play the pattern backwards.)

Next leave out some of the notes within the pattern.

EXAMPLE

Leaving out one note in two groups of four creates groups of seven.

EXAMPLE

Leaving out three notes results in groups of five.

EXAMPLE

Leave out some notes and add rests.

EXAMPLE

As you can see, this approach leads to a very expansive way of hearing sequences.

Ascend or descend within the sequence.

EXAMPLE

Skip up or down to any note in the scale to start the sequence.

EXAMPLE

Try applying polyrhythmic approaches to the sequence.

EXAMPLE

It becomes clear that this approach has infinite possibilities. When practicing these exercises start off with familiarizing yourself with the sequence and then work your way through the possibilities taking as many liberties as you'd like. Try composing 12 modal sequences and then playing each of them on one or more of the play along tracks.

Here is an example of rhythmizing a sequence. The sequence is:

Here is that sequence rhythmized. (Can you follow the sequence through this melody?)

33 Conceptual Practice and Rhythmic Grammar

Most of the material presented in the last few chapters is of a conceptual nature. These approaches can alter your playing profoundly. Here are some other conceptual ideas to consider which can also greatly impact your playing.

- Never start on beat one.
- Never end on beat one.
- Play predominantly eighth notes.
- Play without using eighth notes.
- Anticipate chords by 1/2 beat, by 1 beat, by 1 1/2 beats, by 2 beats, by 2 1/2 beats, by 3 beats.
- Resolve late by 1 beat, 2 beats, 3 beats, or 4 beats.

Learning to pace one's self and to tell a story takes experience. Sometimes players make the mistake of trying to play everything that they have ever learned in one solo. The next solo sounds like a repeat of their last. It takes experience and patience to tell a story and to develop a few ideas.

Leave periods at the ends of sentences and paragraphs. Know when to end your solo. Listen to the rests. The listener will invite your next idea.

In exploring the concepts of this book you can enter the consciousness of discovery where we are all eternal students.